Solving Our Waste: The War on Us

By Troy Betts

Solving Our Waste: The War On Us

Contents

Intro:

Recycling, heralded by most as the pinnacle of waste management. The best we can strive for. But what's happened to recycling? It's all over Facebook, YouTube, and even in the paper and on the news, that trouble is brewing…but what do we really know?

Well, unless you've spent hours upon hours researching like I have, you're probably like the rest of the world and just don't know how dire of a situation we are in with regards to recycling. Some people don't even know there's a problem.

 You have your bin, same as you always have, nothing has likely changed. You still sort your plastics and glass and pop cans…but are you doing the right thing? Well, yes and no.

Throughout this book, we will discuss the pros and cons of recycling. The ups and downs, do's and don'ts, and many other topics.

We'll learn about the challenges facing the world and our society, and what we can do about it. We'll also look at the current and future state of recycling in our communities and lives.

Solving Our Waste: The War On Us

Recycling is a very complicated business, that until recently has had the appearance to many, of being a simple, almost magical process. You would put your plastic water or juice bottle in the recycling bin, and it was magically turned into a new product. At least that's as much interest in the process as most people had.

The reality behind the middle ground, the actual process, is staggering. Your bottle can be transferred to more than 4 or 5 facilities in the sorting process BEFORE it was being shipped to China, where it AGAIN could see 4 or 5 more facilities before it was made into a new product.

In this book, we will go over several of the key aspects to our waste problem at a high level. We will be discussing topics such as:

Elimination

Substitution

Reduction

Reuse

Recycling

Recover

Landfill

In each of these topics, I will provide an easy to understand rundown, and provide personal accounts of how each of these has impacted my life, and yours, whether it's realized or not. By the end of this book, I hope to have peeked your interest in these and further topics.

To get anywhere with recycling, we must first understand the problem. To understand it, we must Define it, and to Define it, we must understand it's history. Let's begin.

A Brief History of Recycling

Recycling has been around since ancient times. Earliest accounts are as far back as 400 BC. Even the Romans recycled bronze coins to make statues that they could sell at higher values. Wartime saw metals and pottery being recycled in hard times.

So, recycling has been around for a very long time. It's not a new concept. In pre- industrial times, materials such as glass and aluminum were recycled into new items. Metals would be melted down, dust and ash from wood and coal fires where used to make bricks.

When industrialization came around, it changed the face of recycling. What was once a necessity for life to exist, or for some people to even make a living, became less of a criticality as it was becoming cheaper and easier to use virgin materials.

During Times of depression, recycling would see some surge, as people needed to make do with what little they had. Many couldn't afford to buy new items, and had to find new ways to use what they had.

Recycling boomed during World War II. Shortages of materials due to the war efforts made it once again vital to recover resources and turn them into new items. Massive campaigns took place worldwide to urge people to donate metals and conserve their fabrics.

Up to this point, recycling was a vital economic need for civilization. After the war, in the 1940's and 50's, landfilling became a cheaper way to dispose of trash. The US, among other countries, largely forgot about recycling, as it was no longer viewed as the cheapest and most efficient way to get rid of our waste.

Recycling was largely ignored for many years, and many people forgot what it even was. In 1953, companies such as Coca Cola and Philip Morris among others, took to creating the Keep America Beautiful campaign with the famous "Crying Indian" commercial, to curb public outcry about the waste they were generating.

This again changed the face of recycling. In 1971, the Keep America Beautiful foundation launched "Earth Day" with the "Crying Indian" PSA release, putting the responsibility of litter and waste control onto the consumer, rather than the corporation.

In 1974, Missouri initiated the first city service for recycling, collecting recycling as they collected municipal waste. This was the beginning of what we know recycling to be today, but for many years, still went rather unnoticed as it was no longer a way of making a living for most people.

In 2006, Al Gore released the documentary "An Inconvenient Truth". While not directed at recycling, it had a major impact as many people started realizing the damage being done to the planet.

In 2017, China announced that they were going to impose strict restrictions around the waste that they would accept. Most people were unaware that China was even taking the majority of our recycling materials, and near the beginning of 2018, news reports started coming out, commenting on the situation.

Once the restriction took effect, recycling centers noticed a major impact to their businesses. Several centers closed, some continue to struggle, some stockpile recycling waste, and some try to search for new countries to ship their waste to.

Many recycling centers continued with their normal collection process, to minimize the impact to the community and their business. Plastic recycling dropped out and lost all of its value on the market. This has caused a stockpile in many of the centers still collecting plastic.

The recycling of carboard has also taken quite a hit, with the market value dropping to roughly $10 per bale at the time of this print. Metal items are expected to remain profitable for the time being, but it's not a guarantee.

Recycling has gone through many changes throughout the years, and is destined to go through many more changes in the future. Now that we've talked a brief history about recycling, and caught up to modern day, let's look at Defining our problem.

Defining the Problem

Just How Big is it?

OK, so we have some history about how recycling has behaved in the past, and we know there's a problem. But just how big of a problem is it? Let's look at some information from the EPA and other sources:

- Over 380 billion plastic bags, sacks and wraps are consumed in the U.S. each year.

- U.S. goes through 100 billion plastic shopping bags annually. (Estimated cost to retailers is $4 billion).

- **The average family accumulates 60 plastic bags in only four trips to the grocery store.**

- Over one million plastic bags are consumed worldwide per minute.

- Plastic bags have been found floating north of the Arctic Circle near Spitzbergen, and as far south as the Falkland Islands

- Scientists estimate that every square mile of ocean contains about 46,000 pieces of floating plastic

- Plastic bags can take up to 1,000 years to break down, so even when an animal dies and decays after ingesting a bag, the plastic re-enters the environment, posing a continuing threat to wildlife.

- The amount of petroleum used to make a plastic bag would drive a car about 115 meters. It would take only 14 plastic bags to drive one mile!

- There is now six times more plastic debris in parts of the North Pacific Ocean than zooplankton. **The Great Pacific Garbage Patch** is twice the size of France.

All this info is strictly about plastic waste. In many communities, plastic is no longer recyclable due to the new restrictions placed on the quality and cleanliness of our recycling. This is a world-wide problem, that affects every nation.

Recent reports have indicated that almost every person on the planet has some level of plastic inside them, and we're not talking from plastic surgery. Every time you eat breakfast, lunch, or dinner, it's likely that you're ingesting small amounts of plastic waste with your food. The reports that every person in the world has plastic inside them is disturbing to me.

The Great Pacific garbage patch is not an Island made of plastic like many people think, but more of a slurry of decaying plastic waste floating in the ocean, with some pieces smaller than a flake of glitter.

In January of 2018, China, our main exporter of recyclable materials placed a ban on many types of waste, including ALL plastics. Why? They were simply being over ran with materials that they couldn't process into new materials, because there was too much contamination in what we were sending them.

While they were accepting almost 90% of our recycling, they were only able to use, LESS THAN 30%. The rest went to their landfills. The contamination was so great, that the Chinese government imposed very tight restrictions on waste import to try and reduce the pollution that was being generated through the import of waste.

So how has that affected the US? There has been a significant impact on our society. Material recovery facilities like your local recycling companies, have been hit hard! The price of materials has dropped significantly, eating away at the company's profits and in some cases, ability to even keep their doors open.

China was our main buyer for recyclable materials, but when their landfills started to become overrun, and the country was being to be polluted heavily with our waste, they had to decide for what was best for them.

They placed heavy restrictions on importing waste, essentially bringing our recycling abilities to a screeching halt. All over the world, recycling is not what we thought it was. It's not the magical process of putting a bottle in a bin, and magically we create a new bottle.

The reality behind the middle ground of the recycling process, the actual process, is staggering. Your bottle can be transferred to more than 4 or 5 facilities in the sorting process BEFORE it was being shipped to China, where it AGAIN could see 4 or 5 more facilities before it was made into a new product.

Some countries have taken to focusing on burning all their waste as opposed to recycling it. Some countries like ours, try to continue with minimal impact to their people. Some are trying to capitalize on the situation and corner the market for waste and recycling Import.

Recycling is in dire straits, and is a problem for every single person in the world. Most people will never know just to what extent the problem presents itself, and some still, will never know that it's a problem at all.

16

Who Does Recycling Affect?

It'd be easy to sit here and say that recycling affects everyone in the whole world, because it does, but I think there needs to be more explanation.

Let's start with a somewhat recent event that happened in 2018, where a whale beached itself and died after ingesting so much plastic waste that it basically starved to death. Think about it, where do whales live? They sure don't live by the shores of third world countries, they live in the ocean. The deep blue sea.

Now there's no telling where it ate all that plastic, or how long it had been inside the poor creature, but it was there, and enough to kill one of the largest animals on earth.

Another incident made headlines in 2018 in July, where thousands of tons of waste washed up on the shores of the Dominican Republic. Hundreds of city workers and volunteers worked to clean up the beaches.

Personal Story: I never really paid any attention to recycling or environmental issues in general until I acquired a new position at my job. Back in 2017, I got a new position that dealt with waste management and recycling operations at the company.

I was inexperienced with environmental issues, but I wanted to do a good job, so I started researching. I researched waste management, recycling, and other issues day in and day out, and quickly realized that I was not the only one at my job that didn't know very much.

Some of the people I worked with on my team had gone thru years of collage to get a degree in environmental sciences...but they were just as lost as I was when it came to recycling. How could that be? They had the education to back it up, so why weren't they miles ahead of me when it came to this?

Well, I did what I do and researched. Their educations were great, and they had fountains of knowledge I didn't have, but, there education stopped. Once they graduated, and got into the workforce, they stopped learning about some things.

While their education on recycling stopped, the flow of knowledge around recycling boomed. It wasn't long before I was informing them of news and new practices in recycling. I found that our company was recycling materials, that our local recycler didn't accept.

We were consistently contaminating our recycling waste stream. I contacted our local recycler and realigned our practices to match with theirs, only to find out a few months later that they changed what they would accept.

So again, I realigned our practices, and again they changed. I was very frustrated at this point and met with our recycler first hand to see what was going on. I found that they weren't just changing the rules to piss me off, they were following the market flow.

If a recyclable material lost its value in the market, the recyclers would have to sort that items out of their collection, before any of the materials could be sold to the next recycler. Because of this, they'd then have to update their acceptance list, which almost nobody was aware even existed.

Solving Our Waste: The War On Us

So, Recycling effects everybody. It effects fish and wildlife, people, businesses, communities, countries, it effects everyone. Most people can't see it for more than the surface sheen that our society has glazed over it, but it's there. It's always been there, and likely always will be there.

How Recycling Works

Recycling is a fantastic concept. Taking something that would be thrown away, and give it new life to make it into an all new product. Eternal life for an eternal waste…maybe not. Recycling in many communities has been heralded as the pinnacle of waste management. But what are we really achieving with recycling, and why is it SO LOW on the pyramid? Not an easy question to answer.

The thought is that "If we place that plastic bottle in the recycle bin, it'll get taken away and made into something else, simple.

" We're saving the planet!" Right? Seems right, you're taking a material that takes hundreds of years to decompose and sending it off to be reused. Open and shut case…Right? Not even close.

There's many questions out there we should be asking ourselves, such as:

1. Do you know what type of plastic the bottle is?
2. Is the bottle stamped with a recycle number?
3. Do you know what that number means?
4. Is there a label on the bottle?
5. Is there a cap on the bottle?

6. Will your recycler accept that bottle?

How do you feel about that bottle after answering these questions? Feeling confident? Here's a couple more:

1. How does your recycler process that bottle?
2. Do they sort it?
3. Do they bale it?
4. Do they ship it to another company?
5. Do they grind it up?
6. Do they burn it?
7. Do they ship it across seas?
8. Do they ship it across the country?

Still confident that your bottle is recycled? Each of these questions can be broken out into many more questions, and we haven't even gotten to what it will be transformed into, which has even MORE questions that can be asked. The list of questions goes on and on and on. So, is it worth it? Just how does it work?

The materials that we recycle and throw into our bins at home are first collected by the areas local recycling center. Depending on the size of the recycle center, our materials take different paths, but they all start the same. Sorting.

Everything is sorted, usually by complicated machines and conveyors, and by hand from the company's employees. Some centers are so small, they sort by hand what they can, bale the materials, and transfer sell to larger facilities that can sort better.

Once sorted, they're baled and shipped, sometimes across the country, to larger recyclers or distribution centers. These companies may yet again sort the incoming material, re-bale the items, and send it across the ocean on a barge or shipping vessel.

"OK, wait. Why do we ship it across the ocean?" Due to many complicated trade factors, it was cheaper for us to send our recycling to China, rather than build the infrastructure to process the materials ourselves.

In January of 2018, China, our main exporter of recyclable materials placed a ban on many types of waste, including ALL plastics. Why? They were simply being over ran with materials that they couldn't process into new materials, because there was too much contamination in what we were sending them.

While they were accepting almost 90% of our recycling, they were only able to use, LESS THAN 30%. The rest went to their landfills. The contamination was so great, that the Chinese government imposed very tight restrictions on waste import to try and reduce the pollution that was being generated through the import of waste.

So how has that affected the US? There has been a significant impact on our society. Material recovery facilities like your local recycling companies, have been hit hard! The price of materials has dropped significantly, eating away at the company's profits and in some cases, ability to even keep their doors open.

But the companies are not giving up. Many continued collections of materials as normal, trying not to impact their local communities, but in doing so, they have stockpiled enormous amounts of waste that have little or no value. Some companies restricted the materials they would accept, but raising the awareness to their customers has been a challenge.

The Waste Hierarchy

So why are we so **BAD** at recycling? Well, did you properly process that Juice bottle that you threw in the recycling bin? No, you did not.

That juice or sports drink bottle first needs to be rinsed, then you need to remove the label, then remove the glue used to adhere the label, then you need to remove the cap and ring, then you need to make sure it's the appropriate resin of plastic for the bin you are placing it in.

Sound a little more complicated? It is, and that's one of the reasons many recovery facilities have developed equipment to try and do that on a mass scale, but it's not 100% effective, and not all facilities have that capability.

So, what are we supposed to do? If we can't recycle, why not burn it for energy? We do, at least as much as we can. Many waste to energy sites are running at or near full capacity, and while they maintain emission levels based on the requirements of their local government, they can still spew out toxic or harmful chemicals, and all that ash has to go somewhere…. Usually straight to landfill.

So, what can I, as the individual user of this disposable plastic item, do to help stem the tide of waste overload? You need to follow the Waste Hierarchy. If you know the waste hierarchy pyramid, and even if you don't, we've all heard Reduce, Reuse, Recycle. While this is generally accepted by ALL as the law of recycling, there's more to it, it's just not as catchy. Eliminate, Substitute, Reduce, Reuse, Recycle, Recover, Landfill.

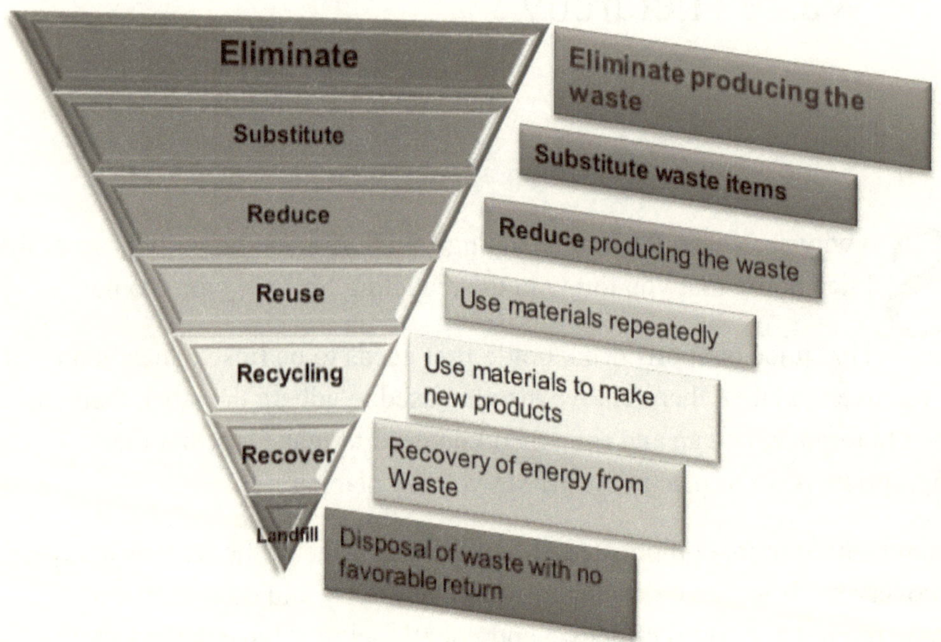

Most people think of recycling as the best thing we can do with our waste, as you can see, it's not even close. While recycling is a good methodology, it's simply too complicated, and we generate too much waste for it to be the main sustainable answer.

The waste hierarchy takes many forms, but they all boil down to the same steps and priorities. The hierarchy pictured above is one that I myself personally created.

Solving Our Waste: The War On Us

While doing my research, the normal waste hierarchies seemed a bit bland. They didn't seem to tell the full story of how we should be looking at our waste, so I expanded.

The normal reduce, reuse, recycle pyramid left a lot of information off. Information that's vital if we want to truly understand our waste and how to overcome our problems.

I've expanded on the hierarchy to include elimination, substitution, waste to energy and landfill. By doing this, we should be able to get a much better understanding of what to do.

Walking the Path

Eliminate Your Footprint

So, what should we really do? Start at the top of the pyramid. Look for single use or waste items that you can **ELIMINATE** from your lives. This isn't as hard as it may sound. If you're about to throw something away, ask yourself this one question, what I call my **Primary Question," Do I need this trash?"**

Do you need that disposable plastic cup when your cabinet is full of glass or ceramic cups, just collecting dust? Do you need those paper plates or plastic forks, just because you don't have to wash them? Then ask yourself this, "How much money is this throw away convenience costing me?"

Personal story: I am a family of five, and before I became entrenched in environmental sustainability, we would buy plastic cups, paper plates, plastic spoons, and plastic forks, simply for the convenience of not having to wash dishes.

I decided to perform a waste analysis on my home and identified the following:

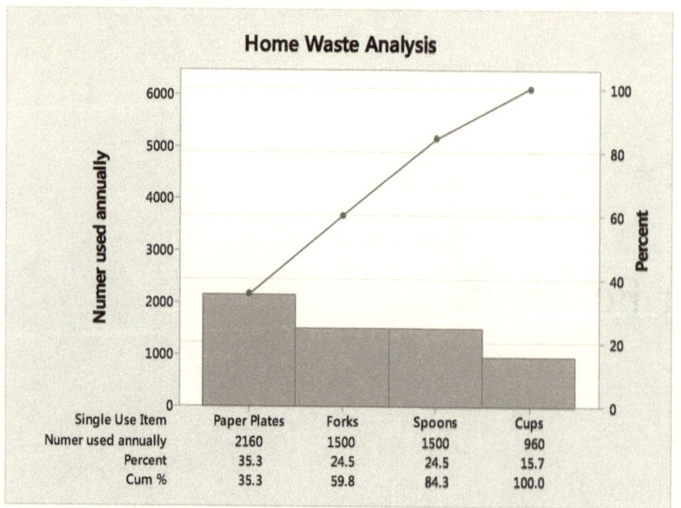

Single Use Item	Paper Plates	Forks	Spoons	Cups
Numer used annually	2160	1500	1500	960
Percent	35.3	24.5	24.5	15.7
Cum %	35.3	59.8	84.3	100.0

We were using over **2000 paper plates** every year because it was "easier"! I took this data and decided to calculate how much money on average I was spending on this convenience…it made me sick.

Paper plates: $240, Plastic Forks: $90, Plastic Spoons: $90, Plastic Cups: $120, Total Annual Cost: $540. Then I started thinking, how much of the garbage I throw away is these items. I started paying attention and found that easily **HALF** of all our trash, was single use items. This led to thinking, if I stop buying this convenience, will my garbage bill go down as well? I haven't taken the plunge yet, but it could.

We could possibly be able to downsize to a smaller garbage can and save $10 a month. So, by eliminating the single use items we generated out of convenience, we're saving on average over $500 a year, or $45 per month, plus the potential for another $120 to put back in our wallet.

There's other things that you can do to eliminate waste as well. Why not buy your meat straight from the butcher case at your local grocer? It's likely to be fresher than the prepackaged meats, wrapped in plastic, and sitting on a Styrofoam tray for days.

Try buying fresh veggies instead of packaged, frozen or canned veggies. The flavor is better, there's more possibilities of how to use the veggies, and there's far less plastic waste involved.

Elimination can play a huge role in your total waste consumption, but how do you know where your waste is?

Like I said earlier, you need to ask yourself questions. When you have an item in your hand, ready to put it in the garbage, as yourself **"Do I need this trash?"**

Elimination can come before we head to the garbage. For instance, when you're in the store, ask yourself if there's a less packaged version of the product your wanting to buy.

Ask yourself if it's something you even need. Do you shop on amazon? If so, build your cart till you have more than one or two items. Shipping multiple items together will cut down on boxes and plastic packaging.

Do you use single use dishware? You just read my story about how much we go through, and how much it costs. Don't narrow your thinking to just plastic. Plastic may be a large part of our daily lives, but it's not the only waste we generate.

Do you get lots of junk mail, or magazines? Do credit card offers flood your mailbox? These days you can stop a lot of the junk mail from coming to you by signing up for online statements.

You can likely get most if not all your bills or even paystubs or reports, online through your email.

Only you know how much waste you generate, and what kinds. Pay attention to what you throw away, and try to find a solution

Substitute Your Life

Step 2 on the hierarchy is **SUBSTITUTE**. This gets a little more attention than elimination, but not enough. What can you substitute? Turns out…just about everything! So, let's start with the obvious big one, plastic bags.

Reusable bags are everywhere and you probably see someone with one every time you go grocery shopping. Heck, you may even have one or two yourself. I used to think that reusable bags where "snobby". That only uptight, pretentious, or radically environmentalist people used them. I was wrong, and if I was right, I'm glad to finally be a part of that club.

Personal story: My wife and I go shopping every Sunday for groceries that we'll need throughout the coming week. We would accept plastic bags because we didn't know any better. We'd get home, and spend 15 minutes unloading bags from the car into the house. Usually a bag would tear on the way and we'd either barely make it in to the house, or have to pick something up off the ground.

The bags were heavy and hard to carry, we'd each throw 6 or 7 bags onto each arm and waddle into the house like drunk penguins, most times having to return to the car to get another load. When we got everything in the house and unloaded, we'd throw our collection of plastic bags on top of the fridge, to be used as bathroom garbage bags.

We generated typically over 20 plastic bags every time we went to the store. When we decided to switch over to reusable bags, we were shocked at the difference. Our groceries that took 20 plastic bags to carry, reduced to only **4**, count them, 4 reusable bags…consistently.

While they are typically heavy, my wife or I can now carry them all, by ourselves, on one arm, in one trip from the car to the house. We don't have to worry about the bags ripping, and as a bonus, we rarely ever see our bread smashed into a ball, like what would happen in a plastic bag.

Sure, we may have paid $15 for 12 bags, but it's SO much easier now to pack around groceries. You could save money by buying bags, as some stores charge you a fee, every time you ask for or accept plastic bags.

So, bags are great, what else? How about freezer and sandwich baggies? Did you know that you can purchase reusable, dishwasher safe zipper baggies?

If you pay $3 for a box of baggies, and you get 3 different sizes like we do, and you need to buy more every 3 months, you're spending $27 bucks a year. Not bad, but considering you can get reusable baggies for under $20 that will last you several years, you can see how it makes more sense to Substitute.

Do you use a lot of plastic wrap? Instead, try beeswax wrap. This cool little product acts like saran wrap but gives you a tighter seal, doesn't bunch up on itself, is reusable, and you can easily rinse it in cold water or use a mild detergent if needed.

I don't know about you, but to eliminate the headache of trying to keep saran wrap from bunching up or sticking to itself, I'd pay almost anything. Luckily, it's less than $20 for a pack. May seem pricey at first, but at $4-$5 a box for saran wrap, you could end up paying the same price or more every year. There's so much out there it's ridiculous, all you have to do is look.

"So where do I look?"

"What do I look for?"

Those questions are not as hard as they may seem. First off, you can find almost anything on Amazon. Love it or hate it, Amazon probably has a substitute item for you.

As to what you look for? I answer that question with another question;

"What do you throw away?"

Remember to ask yourself my **Primary Question, "Do I need this trash?"**

If you're throwing something away, you probably don't. I've talked about dishware before, but I'm going to bring it up again. Paper plates and bowls, plastic cup, forks spoons, and knives, get rid of them!

Stop buying these items! Yes they're convenient, yes you don't have to do the dishes if you don't have any, but if you want to make an immediate and noticeable impact to your garbage, stop. Just stop buying them.

Straws… now here's another biggie. Recently the straw epidemic has surfaced and started causing an uproar. Straws come in handy, and I keep a straw with me at home and at work. A straw. A single straw.

There are many cool straws out there such as bamboo straws, stainless steel straws, and my favorite, silicone straws. Take one of these straws with you when you go out to eat instead of using a disposable plastic straw. Just be warned, people will probably ask you where you got it cause they're awesome and people will want one.

Do you own, run, or work at a restaurant? Paper straws could be a very attractive substitution. Paper straws look and feel cool, and people aren't used to them like they were in the 50's.

You may even get a reputation boost by going to paper. People are going to "feel better" about themselves and your business because you're not using plastic.

It's a small change, but making the customer "feel good" is what it's all about right? If they feel good about your business because you stand out, providing an option to help "save the environment", then they may be more inclined to visit your establishment again just for the paper straws.

The same goes for packaging. If you sell a product that comes double or triple packed…you don't really stand out. However, if you sell a product that comes in a single layer of non-plastic packaging while all your competitors still use plastic packaging, then you **will** start to stand out.

I know I got into the corporate PR aspect for a moment, but I think people go about "confronting" companies the wrong way. People bash, harass, and demonize companies for their packaging, yet go home and use that product anyway.

Refusing to use a product because of its packaging will do nothing, but **choosing** to use a product because of its packaging will do a lot. Choosing a company or product because they use a more innovative packaging than their competitors, will ultimately force their competitors to follow suite.

Companies must get product to the customers in the cheapest, most effective way possible. This usually means plastic, but if we stop focusing on the negatives, and start focusing on the positives, then we'll be able to encourage companies to look at alternatives that will be profitable for them.

Reducing Your Consumption

If you've done things right you should be thinking, "hey, the next step is **REDUCE**, didn't I already do that?" Yup, you sure did. But if I had just told you to reduce you're waste, you'd ask me "How?" and I'd have to explain this all again. By breaking it out, we now have much simpler and hopefully clearer steps to take in achieving the first and most crucial R. If we don't create the waste in the first place, we don't have to recycle it. Starting to make a bit more sense?

So "why is Reduce still in the pyramid?" Because now you're at the point where you need to look at what wastes you generate that you can't eliminate OR substitute, but that you may be able to reduce your generation of. NOW, you've finally made it to the first step of the normal waste hierarchy!

Hold up…" Why is the highest step in the pyramid the first? Shouldn't you start at the bottom and work up?" Nope. When trying to get your waste under control, you need to start at the most stringent process in the system, which just so happens to have the greatest impact on your waste. Hence the upside-down pyramid, and why you need to "walk down the steps".

There's several ways to reduce the amount of waste you're producing, but the biggest one that I'm going to talk about is FOOD.

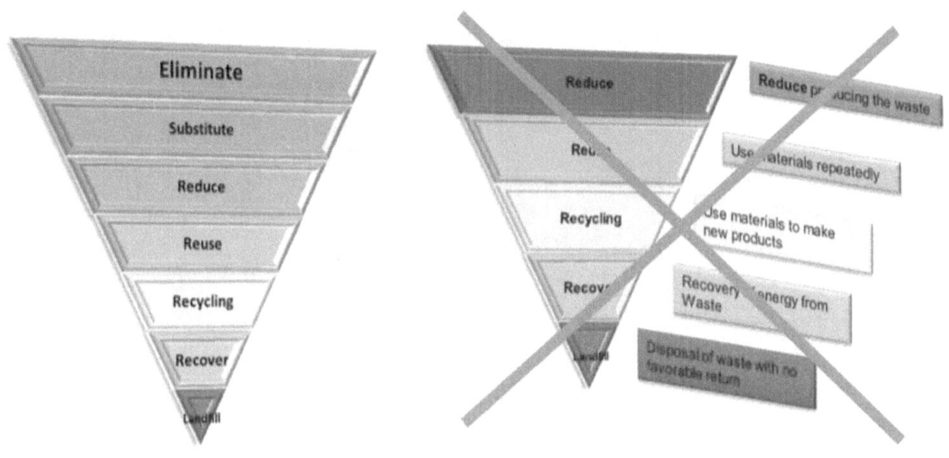

F ood waste is the deceitful bigger sibling to plastic waste. What do I mean by this? Well, it's been estimated that up to one fifth of the food in America is sent to landfills, averaging at about 130 pounds a year per person! MATH TIME!

As of January 1st, 2018, the US population was 327,908,413. If the average waste of each person is 130 pounds per year, how many pounds end up in the landfills? Easy multiplication here, but it comes out to a staggering 42,628,093,690!!! Over 42.5 BILLION pounds a year! How is that even possible!!!

There's a lot here to consider. On the surface, it sounds like just stop throwing away food, but that's not the extent of it. As with all our waste problems, we need to fully understand the problem in its entirety.

This is not a simple task, so let's do the best we can, and start at the source. Where do we get our food?

It all starts at the farm. Farms produce an enormous amount of food waste. Why? Because we as a society are picky, and don't want to buy food products that don't look absolutely pristine. Estimates vary, but generally over 40% of all food produced is wasted at the farm level, because it won't sell due to some minor visual defect.

I'm only talking about food that **IS still** fit for human consumption, but never even hits the store shelves. We see estimates similar to this at the production, retail, AND consumption levels! Ask yourself a question, have you ever passed up a bruised apple, a can of veggies, or a box of food, simply because the packaging was dinged, dented, or a little bit crushed?

If you answer no, I'm going to call you out on it right now. I myself have passed up perfectly edible food just because the packaging wasn't in perfect condition. Items like these are typically pulled from the shelves because the stores know that the chances of selling the item are slim. Stores sell items at very quick rates, so they can't let food just "Hang Out" hoping someone will buy it.

It's not the stores fault, it's not the farms fault, and it's not the manufactures fault…it's our fault. We've become so picky with what we are willing to purchase, that we have created a wasteful society. So how do we reduce our waste? We don't necessarily need to buy less, we need to buy "smarter".

How far out do you plan your meals? Do you buy everything at one time, or throughout the week? Do you buy extra, or only what you think you will eat? There's many more questions that I can ask, but instead, let's have another story time.

Personal Story: As mentioned before, my wife and I shop every week for groceries. We plan out our meals in advance so we only have to go to the store once. Inevitably, we would throw away bags of uneaten veggies or fruits because they started to wilt or go bad, before the planned date for eating the items.

This was annoying because we would then have to make an emergency trip to the store to replace the items so we could stick to our dinner plans. After a while, we decided to start eating the bagged veggies such as salad, earlier in the week, so it wouldn't go bad on us.

This limited us on what we could buy, and what we could have for dinner, and stuff still went "bad" before we could eat them. We hadn't solved our problem, only made it worse. So, then we decided to only buy those "sensitive" items no more than 2 days before we planned to have them for dinner.

We stopped having to throw away as much food, but still didn't solve our purchasing problem. We still would have the occasional bag of spinach start to wilt before we could use it, and sometimes we'd switch a dinner up and something would start going "bad", and we'd throw it out. we still hadn't solved anything.

Then I decided to ask myself, "is what we're throwing away really bad?" I started thinking about our bags of spinach. If some of the leaves started to look wilted or a little brown in the bag, we'd throw it out. But what happens to spinach leaves when you cook them? They wilt.

We almost always cook our spinach simply because we like it better that way. We were throwing away perfectly fine spinach just because it "didn't look good". It was still perfectly edible, but we'd throw an entire unopened bag in the garbage, just because 1 or 2 leaves looked a little wilted.

Since this, we hardly ever throw away spinach or many other veggies just because they don't look pristine. However, like many others, we still have a hard time with the visual. We're not throwing away unopened bags anymore, but still on occasion throw away some individuals that look sketchy.

The Wasteful Process

The food industry is full of waste. With billions of pounds of food either never hitting our plate or being thrown away, you'd think our streets would be overflowing with rotten fruits and veggies, so why aren't they?

Most farms and companies try to minimize the waste that they generate. Farms typically feed the waste food that would never sell in the market, to livestock, or compost some of it to provide nutrition for the next round of crops.

Many companies will return or sell back undesirable food products to the producers to use for composting or livestock feed. This generates a bond between the business and the supplier, and reduces their cost of having to dispose of that waste.

Sounds like a good system, and in many cases, it can be. "So why am I still calling it waste?"

When farmers grow the crop, they put in a LOT of resources to make the product. They must till and clean the area of weeds and non-desirable plant growth, fertilize the area, keep the crop watered, and keep it pruned in some cases. Farmers spend a lot of time managing the growth of their crop so that they can spend even more time harvesting and setting up with a buyer to sell the crop.

I'm not a farmer, nor do I believe I ever could be (it's too much hard work for me), but I do know several farmers and cattle ranchers who put in insanely long hours every day just to make a living.

Companies can run the gambit from a big corporation that contracts with a local supplier, sending trucks to pick up product from the farms, to small mom and pop farm to table restaurants that work with their local growers daily to provide the freshest food possible to their customers.

Regardless of the type of company, it takes a great deal of time and money to obtain the food product, be it fruit, vegetable, or meat. Therefore, any food that doesn't sell is considered waste.

Farms and companies recoup as much of their loss as possible by turning it into livestock feed or compost, but they make no profit on this. Most places don't grow the food with the goal of turning it into livestock feed, they intend to sell it.

Buying from your local farmers market is a great way to get around the company costs, and reduce some of the waste, but there's still one significant issue that plagues our society, appearance.

As mentioned before, if it doesn't look good, people won't buy it. It will sit on the shelf, perfectly edible, until it's pulled and thrown away, or rots.

Personal Story: Years ago, I worked at a cherry cannery. Every day we would get a several truckloads of pie cherries direct from the farm. We would wash them, pit them, sort out the ones that had blemishes, and then package them.

The sorting process saw around 30 people sitting beside conveyor belts, pulling off cherries that either still had a pit, or looked "bad". While the work day was only 5 hours, we would throw away up to a TON of cherries every night. 2,000 pounds of cherries because they didn't "look right".

This was before I became involved with waste, but I still remember thinking, "What a waste. I'd eat all of that if it wasn't garbage." But what made it garbage? The only reason most of it was thrown away was because it was either crushed, had a pit, or had a few black spots that were just bruised skin.

It was still ALL perfectly edible. I asked what they did with all those cherries and was told that they return them to the farm and use them as livestock feed.

So, we've talked about the farms, and companies that package and sell foods, but there's one bigger waster at the center of all of this, grocery stores. Store throw out a staggering amount of food every day, and unlike with other companies, rarely does that waste food go anywhere but the trash.

Some stores sell meat scraps to local butchers at a massively reduced price, it not outright donating the scraps. Some stores work with local food banks and homeless shelters to try and offload food that will no longer sell, but is still edible.

Some stores don't have the ability to do this, and are left with no choice but to throw the food away. Still perfectly edible food for the most part, but it just won't sell.

This is where "dumpster divers" come in. There's a lot of controversy around dumpster diving and the legality around it, but the Abandonment of Property principle states that if property "is found in a place where the true owner likely intended to leave it, but is in such a condition that it is apparent that he or she has no intention of returning to claim it, it becomes the property of whoever should find it and take possession of it first"

That's a mouth full, but basically, if it's in the dumpster, it's up for grabs, just don't trespass on private property please. Many businesses will lock up their dumpsters to keep people out because they're afraid of being liable if the diver is injured. The truth behind that though, is if your diving, you and you alone are responsible for your actions. If you get hurt diving, that's on you buddy.

Another issue companies have with divers is property damage. Business owners don't want to walk in in the morning to trash all over their parking lot, or their bins broken to pieces. They don't want to have to clean all that up, or replace something if you break it, would you?

Dumpster diving can be good for the environment, and profitable for the diver, but within reason. You don't want to make a bigger mess by diving. If you want to dive, I'd recommend talking to the business owner FIRST, and discuss a sort of contract where you come in after hours, and leave the area the way you found it. You may not get many takers, but if just a few take you up on the offer, it could be beneficial for you, the business, and the environment.

The Expiration Date Conundrum

All my research into waste led me to looking into expiration dates on items, and I quickly realized, I had it all wrong.

I, like many others, thought that the expiration printed on my food item was for me. I thought it was telling me that once it hit this magical date, it was no longer fit for human consumption. I thought that if it was expired, it'd make us sick if we ate it. Wrong wrong wrong….

Those dates on the can of corn or jar of salsa weren't for me, they're for the store. Those dates are there to tell the store how often they should rotate their stock, not when the food goes bad. I did research and found that there are multiple types of expiration dates generally used. If you take anything away from reading all this, take the following section PLEASE!

Let's look at some of the more common expiration dates here.

Sell by: The labeling "sell by" tells the store how long to display the product for sale. And is basically a guide for the retailer, so the store knows when to pull the item. The "sell by" date is the last day the item is at its highest level of quality (according to the manufacturer), but it will still be edible for some time after.

Best if used by or before: This refers strictly to quality, not safety. This date is recommended for best flavor or quality (again, according to the manufacturer). It is not a purchase or safety date.

Use by: This is the last date recommended for the use of the product while at peak quality. The date has been determined by the manufacturer of the product.

None of these dates are a "drop dead" date, but the **Use By** date is the closest.

Some items such as baby formula have an "Expiration" date, but general food items have typically one of the three listed above. Those labels are not telling you that it's safe to eat the food ONLY before that date, they tell you when the item is at peak flavor, and may start to deteriorate in looks or flavor. It's also good to note that these dates are ONLY valid until the product packaging is opened. So, let's take milk as an example.

Personal Story:

We go thru a lot of milk in our family, at least a couple gallons a week, so the "expiration" never really bothered us. However, I always noticed that the expiration on the plastic milk jug was never more than 3-5 days out. We decided to switch to carton milk for the flavor, and to reduce the amount of plastic waste we generated, and I noticed that the date on the carton was sometimes 2-3 WEEKS out.

This confused me. How could the same milk have such a large difference in time for when it "went bad"? (It all depends on the pasteurization process) We made the switch and I did what I have grown accustom to doing, and researched my question.

I found the difference between the pasteurization processes, and what the dates on the containers mean? They're still only a guideline for when it's at peak flavor. The milk can last longer, but there's no guarantee of freshness after this point.

I asked myself "So how can I tell if the milk has gone bad?" The answer? First, smell it. If it smells fine and doesn't have any sour or funky smell, then taste it. If you're worried about getting sick, don't do it (it's doubtful you'd get sick, but if you're worried, safety first). I've done the smell and taste test with many food items now and have never gotten sick. I have however found a few things that didn't taste quite right, and discarded them.

Understanding the dates that are on our food is one of the biggest steps to reducing our waste. We throw away too much perfectly edible food because it either doesn't look pristine, or because we see a date and think the food is "Expired" after that point.

So how do you reduce your food waste? Simple, buy less if you can, and taste it before you throw it out. If you want to be able to make any amount of change, you must take the responsibility upon yourself to make the right decision.

I can't prevent the farms from throwing away good food because of aesthetics, but I can be a little less picky, and a lot smarter in what I buy. Just because that box of stuffing is a little crunched on one corner, doesn't mean it's no good. Just because that "sell by" date is about to elapse, doesn't mean that pasta is about to go stale, or that the milk has gone sour. You must inform yourself about the issue before you make a change, otherwise, you could **make a change for the worst**.

Let's look at a few food items that commonly get "thrown out" because the date elapsed or it doesn't look perfect.

Milk: I know, I've droned on about milk several times, but with the short sell by dates that usually accompany the container, a lot of milk goes to waste and gets poured down the sink.

Smelling your milk should be the FIRST thing you do when you question the freshness. **Does it have a sour smell?** If yes, I'd say better safe than sorry and dump it. If no, taste it. Unless you have a compromised immune system, a little taste is not likely make you sick. If it tastes fine, then I personally make the decision to go ahead and consume it. Again, make your own choice.

Beef: We've all had this issue (if you eat meat) that you pull something out of the freezer or fridge, and it's got a brown tinge to it. Maybe you've gotten some nice pink burger, and just under the top layer, it looks like it's already been cooked.

This doesn't mean that the burger is rotten or spoiled. A variety of factors can cause the meat to look unappealing, such as diet, breed, exercise, age, light exposure and if it's been frozen. Smell it, if it smells fine, touch it, as long as it's not slimy or sticky outside of what it normally feels like, it should be fine.

Cheese: Many people know this already, but I'll mention anyway. Cheese is a miraculous product, and even if it has some mold on it, it's still consumable. Just cut the mold off. Again, the visual is hard for lots of people to get past, and a lot of cheese get thrown away because of mold.

Expiration dates don't, or shouldn't, mean much to us, the consumer. They're there for the most part to tells stores when to rotate their stock. We as a society, are not good with the visual, and have taken "expiration" dates to mean the last day we can safely consume a product.

But think of one more thing here to hopefully help you wrap your mind around this concept. When you buy a package of meat, it typically has a sell by date that will elapse within the next three to five days, but when you get it home, you may freeze it for months before using it.

You've long elapsed that date, but you use it anyway. That's because those dates are not "magical" drop dead dates. Your eyes are deceitful little creatures when it comes to food. Just because it looks bad, doesn't mean it is.

Reusing What You Paid For

Reuse is much simpler than some of the other steps. It literally is about reusing an item rather than throwing it away. Sometimes it can be difficult to come up with ways to reuse an item, or find benefit in doing so. There's all sorts of nifty crafts on YouTube on how to reuse or repurpose plastic items, but not everyone is craft minded.

Whether your crafty or not, it's easy to reuse something, and we do it all the time without even noticing. Have you ever rinsed out a solo cup so you could use it again? Ever use that plastic grocery bag to put your bathroom garbage in?

Just about everything you have or generate can be reused as something else, and every time you reuse something, it's the equivalent of not generating the waste of the newly purposed item. But this is still waste. Let me explain.

If you go shopping and accept 10 plastic bags, and use those bags to line your bathroom garbage, you eliminated the generation of 10 garbage bags, but still generated 10 shopping bags. Let's get a little craftier.

You finish off the last of that gallon jug of milk and your dog whines cause he's hungry. You go to scoop him some food and remember that man's best friend got a hold of the scoop recently and chewed it to oblivion. Being a crafty person, you cut a scoop out of the milk jug, and use it for months to feed your furry friend.

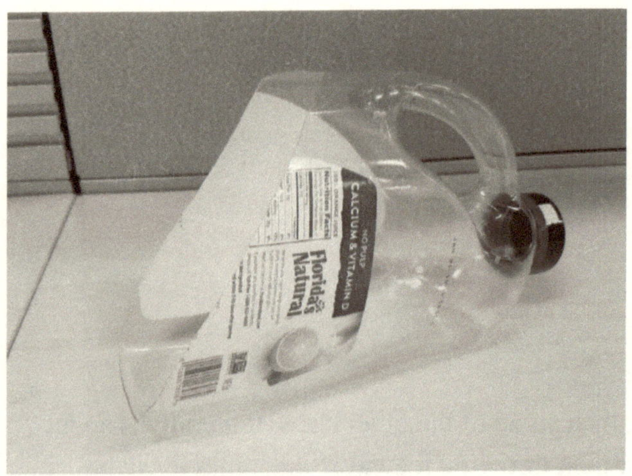

You've reused that milk jug, or part of it. But it's still there, you still wasted half of the jug, and eventually the makeshift scoop will fail, and you'll have to replace it again. While it may not be a 1 for 1 ratio, in the end you are still generating a waste to eliminate a waste.

Not the worst of options, but it's less effective to simply reuse a waste, than to eliminate, substitute, or reduce the waste generation. You're only limited by your imagination on how to reuse a waste, but in order to reuse a waste, you must FIRST generate the waste.

Personal Story: I'm a crafter. I like to make things, and one of the things I like to make, are "Damnit Doll" style dolls that I call **"Wasted Dolls"**.

Why do I call them that? Simple, I only use materials that were destined for the landfill in the creation of the dolls. I take strips of tattered, worn, or otherwise ruined clothing, and cut out my dolls. I then stuff my dolls with plastic bags or packaging that again, are destined for the landfill.

I do this as not only a way to "reuse" plastic waste, but also to entertain my children. My kids LOVE the dolls! They're durable, flexible, soft, and pretty cute. My kids can be as rough as they want with the dolls, slamming them on the ground, beating each other up, throwing, kicking, punching, etc. And best of all, it's cheap.

Granted I have to put quite a bit of time into the design and fabrication of the doll, sometimes a couple days, but cost of materials is low. Sometimes I'll spend a few bucks at the thrift store for an old pair of pants no one will ever want to wear, but it's still not a lot.

My kids are constantly asking me to make more. My kids love them, my coworkers love them, and all the while, it's helping me to reduce the amount of waste I produce at my home.

I ran a challenge at my day job, challenging my coworkers to share a picture of something they reused. A simple task, but it got people thinking. I shared the pictures at work and it generated a lot of buzz.

People started passing back and forth different ideas, and helping others to come up with ways to reuse something they were about to throw out. One person made a reusable bag out of HUNDREDS of plastic grocery bags.

One of the coolest things in my opinion that was shared, was someone simply cutting a plastic bottle and milk jug in half, then putting it over their flowers as a type of individual greenhouse cover to prevent their flowers from freezing in the night.

Another person put down a layer of cardboard under their topsoil to prevent weeds, and allow the plants to grow unhindered. People are inventive, that's the great thing about us. Invention is the mother of necessity as the saying goes, and it couldn't be truer.

Recycling: Half Way Down

We've finally walked down the first half of the hierarchy, and have made it to the problem child. **Recycling**. Like I've mentioned previously, recycling is a fantastic concept. Taking something that would be thrown away, and give it new life to make it into an all new product. Eternal life for an eternal waste…maybe not.

Recycling in many communities has been heralded as the pinnacle of waste management. But what are we really achieving with recycling, and why is it SO LOW on the pyramid? Not an easy question to answer.

The thought is that "If we place that plastic bottle in the recycle bin, it'll get taken away and made into something else, simple.

" We're saving the planet!" Right? Seems right, you're taking a material that takes hundreds of years to decompose and sending it off to be reused. Open and shut case…Right? Not even close.

There's many questions out there we should be asking ourselves, such as:

1. Do you know what type of plastic the bottle is?
2. Is the bottle stamped with a recycle number?

3. Do you know what that number means?
4. Is there a label on the bottle?
5. Is there a cap on the bottle?
6. Will your recycler accept that bottle?

How do you feel about that bottle after answering these questions? Feeling confident? Here's a couple more:

7. How does your recycler process that bottle?
8. Do they sort it?
9. Do they bale it?
10. Do they ship it to another company?
11. Do they grind it up?
12. Do they burn it?
13. Do they ship it across seas?
14. Do they ship it across the country?

Still confident that your bottle is recycled? Each of these questions can be broken out into many more questions, and we haven't even gotten to what it will be transformed into, which has even MORE questions that can be asked. The list of questions goes on and on and on. So, is it worth it?

Personal Story: As mentioned, my wife and I switched to carton milk for the flavor and ability to recycle the carton. We thought this was a significant way to reduce our single use plastic waste. We were wrong, and right.

The cartons we switched to still have plastic. The spout on the side, and the freshness seal, both plastic. So ok, we can cut those out and still recycle the carton, wrong. The cartons are lined with a waxed coating to prevent the milk from seeping through the cardboard, and to help maintain freshness.

On top of this, our recycler, like many others, only takes "corrugated" cardboard (i.e. Shipping boxes). So, what just happened? Well, we ended up paying twice the price for the same amount of milk, reduced our plastic waste, but didn't eliminate like we thought we would. AND, actually increased the bulk of our waste as I measured the surface area of our milk jug vs cartons.

So, wait, we tried to do the right thing to reduce our waste, but actually increased it? Yup. We didn't know until it was too late. We had been getting carton milk for months before I asked the question of can this be recycled, and researched it, only to find the unfortunate answer. Nope.

Let's switch gears and go back to drink bottles. Let's follow the process of a bottle destined for great things.

First things first, you're thirsty, you need a drink, so you grab your bottle of juice. Once it's empty you toss it in the recycling bin. The bin is picked up and your bottle is taken to a local recycling company.

The recycling company puts it on a conveyor belt which sorts it with other like materials and baled. The bottle is sent to (in many cases) a larger facility where it is sorted better and sometimes rinsed. The bottle is then baled with like materials and transported, sometimes across the country to a costal recycling facility or port. The bottle is then loaded onto a boat and shipped across the ocean to China…or at least it was.

With all this effort to get it to China for processing, do you notice something missing from this process? Your bottle was sorted, and somctimes rinsed…but what about the cap, ring, and label?

In most cases, this is where China came in. they would collect all the incoming waste, re-sort the wastes, then transport to a facility that ground the bottles, labels and all, into tiny shreds called grind.

The "grind" would float thru a solution that allowed the plastic from the bottles to sink, but cause "most" of the label and cap grind to float, where it was skimmed off and discarded as trash.

The grind, which was mostly bottles, was then sold to another company where they melted it into pellets. The pellets were then sold to another company that melted and processed the pellets into polyester fiber. The fiber was then sold to companies and made into clothing…

That's quite a long trip for one little bottle. Not to mention the dangers involved with every step of the process, which I won't get into.

This process doesn't always hold true for every bottle, some companies are able to do multiple tasks at one facility, but more than likely, your bottle got some mileage. Going thru this process has many challenges.

Your plastic bottle is 1 in over **50 BILLION** bottles used in the US each year!!! It takes **17 MILLION** barrels of oil to produce that many bottles and we consume over 1500 bottles **PER SECOND!!!** On top of that you have transportation fees, processing fees, carbon footprint, virgin material cost vs recovered materials cost, and less than 30% of those bottles are ever even recycled.

So far, we've only managed to talk about plastic drink bottles. How many other plastic items can you think of?

Personal Story: Early in 2018, I went on a "field trip" with a coworker and several representatives of my local recycling center. The trip was focused on viewing the processes of each of the waste management services in the area.

What I found shocked and amazed me as to the robustness and shear speed of their processes. Garbage was collected from homes and buried in the landfill, within a 16 HOUR timeframe!

I was shocked with the speed of the process, but then I asked about recycling… The response was less than encouraging.

Our local recycler was only able to take a few types of items, cardboard, metals, and some paper, but they don't make a profit.

 The recycler has 2 paid employees, and rely on donations and volunteers to keep their gates open. But why? Turns out, that with the China issue, the market bottomed out for recycling.

Plastic lost all of its value, cardboard dropped from $100 or more a ton, to $10 a ton, glass lost most of its value, metal, while holding steady for now, could expect to see a similar decline in value.

But we still haven't gotten to the bottom of it, why did recycling lose its value? Due to the process involved in recovering materials, it's cheaper and potentially LESS harmful to the environment to use raw or "virgin" material, rather than recovered material.

So yes, in theory recycling is a great methodology, but until the infrastructure around the world can keep up with the output of waste and recyclable products, in a cheap and effective manner, and we're able to "clean up" our act, recycling is just not sustainable, and is not the cure all for our waste problems.

Now would be a great time to start drafting that hate mail about how I'm anti-recycling, and trying to impede saving the planet, but recycling alone won't get us to where we need to go.

Recycling is simply a small little cog in the giant wheel of our waste.

Recovering the Wasteful Losses

So, we've discussed the three R's, Reduce, Reuse, Recycle, but we haven't made it to the bottom of the hierarchy just yet. If I threw you for a loop with recycling, hold onto your britches, cause here it comes again.

Recover… When we talk about recover, we typically think waste to energy, or burning our trash…and that's as deep as we think about it.

We think that everything we could potentially produce, can just get burned and go away forever, leaving a nice clean process. Sorry, but like with everything else waste management, it's just not that simple.

Everything burns at a different temperature, but most of it burns well below the temp in a waste to energy site. Metals on the other hand, do not, and in some cases, need to be sorted out before being processed.

Another issue with waste to energy is emissions. Greenhouse gas emissions are a hot topic anytime the term waste to energy is brought up. Most facilities however, take this very seriously, and go to great lengths to prevent harmful emissions.

Despite all their best intentions however, there is still a certain level of release, and it takes a LOT of energy to create new energy. Transforming heat into electricity is a process.

OK, so sounds great. Shouldn't this be higher up the pyramid? One major issue keeps it low, ash. The ash from the process needs to go somewhere, so where does it go? Straight to a landfill.

Another point that keeps it low on the totem pole, is the fact that if you burn and destroy the product to make energy, there's no recovery of the material. Those virgin materials used to manufacture that bottle, are lost to the ages.

Solving Our Waste: The War On Us

Let's switch gears a little and start talking COMPOST. Ahhh compost. Everyone's go to for the food waste problem. Return the uneaten food to the earth to grow a-new.

Composting is everywhere. People do it in their backyard, some companies or recovery facilities do it in a large yard, some even do it on an industrial scale with huge equipment and fermenters.

Again, another process that sounds great, but again, **why** is it not higher on the list? You're still generating a waste, and putting energy and materials into its creation, just to destroy it and start the process all over again is just wasted resources.

Don't get me wrong, composting is great, but it's very easy to contaminate a compost pile, and not even know it. If you don't have strict controls on what goes into your compost pile, and when, you're going to end up with a mess that could be a potential breeding ground for pests or harmful bacteria.

Composting is a solution to a portion of the waste problem, but is very limited in what it can control. You can't throw a blown tire in the compost pile and expect it to decompose.

Personal Story: I decided I wanted to try making my own compost pile, so I researched what I needed to do, what I could throw into it, how often I needed to turn it, and so on.

I thought, "ok, I've got this, no problem." I watched what I threw into the pile, added my browns and my greens at what I thought was the correct ratio, and for the first couple weeks, I thought I was doing good.

But then, somewhere along the way, I must have begun adding more green material then I was supposed to, or my materials were not correct, or small enough to decompose at a steady rate.

Whatever the reason, before long, my pile started to get a vile smell, the grass around the area began to die, and the interior of the pile turned to a foul-smelling sludge, riddled with maggots.

I still can't figure out what I did wrong, but I did something VERY wrong. Something got put in there that shouldn't have. While I've since cleaned up the area, I still have a patch of dirt where NOTHING will grow. Somehow, I contaminated the area.

I'm not a composter, I'm not good at it, but lots of people are. For some people it's a no brainer and just second nature to compost, but just as some people are not crafters like me, I'm not a composter.

Recovering materials is obviously a better option than throwing something in the garbage, but it takes a lot of work and dedication. Sometimes it can be a hazardous process. It destroys, in order to create. Just like everything else in the pyramid, Recover is not a standalone solution to our waste problem.

Landfills: The History of Us

L et's move on from how bad I suck at composting, to the bottom of the pyramid, LANDFILL! That horrible landfill, contaminating our water and environment! Or is it? Landfills in the US have come a long way in the last 30 years. So, what do we know about landfills?

Personal Story: During my field trip to the local waste management facilities, I got to tour the local landfill. Going in, I was expecting mounds and mounds of garbage, rats or other pests running rampant, and horrible garbage smells…There was none of that.

What I witnessed didn't seem real. There were rolling hills with bright green grass and vegetation, no pests anywhere to be found, and a mild, pleasantly sweet smell in the air that was at times hard to even notice.

On the tour I learned many things. The first thing I learned was that the waste was packed down in layers, covered with specific materials, and layered again till the mound reached the desired size, EVERY DAY. It was then topped with soil and grass seed once it reached the desired size.

Next, I learned that during the packing process, they install seepage canals to control waste water runoff so it wouldn't contaminate the ground water. They also install vent tubes in key areas to prevent methane buildup. The methane released is burned to prevent it from escaping to the atmosphere.

Nothing I witnessed was negligent. The entire process revolved around minimal impact to the environment, but in the end, it's still a landfill, where we simply (not so simply) bury our garbage. There was one more thing I learned that really threw me for a loop.

Stuff in the landfill doesn't decompose! At least not at the normal rate. During an excavation, one of the operators had uncovered a newspaper from 1970, that was still legible and in near mint condition. Newspaper! On top of that, (or underneath it as we were told) the operator had also found a leaf of green lettuce.

The paper is one thing, but green lettuce?! Nearly **50 years later!?** When I asked how it was even possible, the tour guide informed us that as part of their process, they maintain an oxygen deficient atmosphere. This prevents the possibility of fires or explosions, but also doesn't allow for bacteria to grow, and cause decomposition to happen.

Landfills are everywhere, and essential to society, but get a bad rap because of the nature of the business. Just think where we'd be without them. Are there better ways to manage our waste then to send them to a landfill? Most definitely, but landfills serve a very important purpose.

Landfills go to great lengths to ensure the safety of the environment, and the people who live within them. Landfills have come a long way from the eyesores of old.

They tell a story, a history of our consumerism. A history of our lives. Historians dig up ancient landfills to learn more about societies long since passed.

Waste management may seem like a pain at times. Whether it's cost of services, allowable items for disposal, or issues with that extra garbage can blocking your view, waste management is a difficult *and* a much-needed service.

Landfilling is a business, and a very important one at that. On the field trip, I learned that once picked up from my home, my garbage was transported to a collection facility.

At this facility, my garbage was mixed with everyone else's garbage before being transported to the landfill. This facility was amazing. They took in 600 yards of garbage per week.

But that's not the amazing part, the amazing part is that garbage taken in averages only 20 **MINUTES** on the floor before being loaded into a bin and sent to landfill!

I also learned that anything that was in my garbage can when picked up that morning, was in the ground and covered by the end of the day! The speed and efficiency to which the company handled the waste was truly inspiring.

Landfills are important, and yes, not every landfill is created equal. Some landfills have been too close to a source of water and washed away, only to wind up on a beach somewhere down the way.

Anything we can do to keep waste out of the landfills, we should do. Otherwise, historians may one day dig up waste that you once held in your hand.

65

The Next Steps

The Big Question

So, we've finally walked down the hierarchy pyramid, learned a few things, made a few people angry, shared some wins, shared some failures. But just what type of waste have we been talking about, and is there different types? We've been specifically talking about what's in your garbage can at home.

We haven't even begun to touch on industrial waste, medical waste, manufacturing waste, construction waste, bio-waste, haz-waste, etc. There's so many types of waste, and while they all intertwine at some point, they all come with specific and unique challenges.

So how do we solve our waste problem? That is the title of this little book after all, you expect answers. You need answers. You WANT answers. The answers simple, but immensely difficult at the same time. Use your brain.

Seriously? After all this, all I'm giving you is three little words? What the $#%@!

Think about this, I can sit here and tell you till I'm blue in the face what to recycle, how to recycle, what you can live without, what you can substitute, what you can burn, but I **can't** do it for you. No one can. You have to use your brain to learn about what **you** can do, and you have to make that conscious decision to take action.

There is no 1 right answer EXCEPT, think… You've made it this far with all my yammering's, because you wanted to know more. Now you know more. And like it or not, now you have a better understanding of how to fix our waste problem.

Use the waste hierarchy to your advantage. Start at the top and walk down the steps. Ask yourself if there's items you don't need. Are those solo cups just a convenience so you don't have to wash a glass?

If so, why do you have that glass? It's just sitting collecting dust and taking up space. Is it worth your time to put it in the dishwasher to save $120 a year on plastic cups?

That bottle of pop, can you substitute that for a box of cans? You might make some money back by recycling the cans, and the box might be a good way to light that camp fire at your next get together.

Follow the steps, ask the questions, find the answers, but there's one important question you need to ask, that may even be more important than the title question. Why? Why is it important to you?

I can't stress this question enough. If you don't have a personal to yourself reason for why reducing your waste is important, you'll never succeed. Don't just sit there and tell me "because it's good for the environment". That's a bullshit response, and it's not good enough. You'll never stick with it if it's not personal.

Why is it **PERSONAL** to you?

Maybe you want your kids to live in a beautiful, waste free utopia. Maybe you want to save money. Maybe you just want to look more environmentally friendly. Whatever the reason, make sure it's personal to **You.** I found why it was personal to me. All those personal stories are there for a reason. They're personal.

Solving Our Waste: The War On Us

I want to save money! It may not seem like a lot to most people, but $500 a year is a nice little return for honestly doing very little. Putting a dish in the dishwasher doesn't take much effort, and I was going to use the dish soap anyway.

Sometimes I don't even have to put it in the dishwasher, and can just rinse it. A quick rinse right after I use it is sufficient for me. I'm cheap and frugal. I like to save money and cut costs.

My kids are important to me. I want to make sure they don't grow up with trash littering the streets or parks where they play. I appreciate the beauty of my community, and want to keep appreciating.

Then there's the public eye aspect. I have no problem admitting that I feel ashamed to throw away anything in the garbage, let alone just throw it on the ground.

The whole intent of this book is to inform you about our waste situation, and get you to think for yourself, about yourself, and YOUR impact on waste. Ask yourself questions, and put in a little effort to find the answers. Still need a little guidance? Ask yourself these questions, and you may find your answers:

Do I need this?

Is this just a convenience?

Does this cost me more than other options?

Are there less wasteful options out there?

Can I use this more than once?

Can I recycle this?

Can I compost this?

Does my area burn for energy, or ship to somewhere that does?

Is this going to outlive me in the landfill?

Not one step in the pyramid by itself is going to solve the waste problem, it takes all of them working together to make a difference, just like it takes every one of us working together, and that can only happen if you use your brain. If you want to see an immediate and satisfying difference, here's my recommendation:

1. Stop buying single use dishware such as cups, bowls, plates, straws and utensils
   AND
2. Get 4 or 5 reusable bags for your grocery shopping

These two actions alone can make a significant impact on your garbage can **AND** your wallet. If neither of these apply to you, just ask the questions, and use your brain. I never understood it before, but now I know what a certain blue superhero really meant when he said, **"The Power is Yours!"**

Making a Plan

Now that we have some information, some knowledge, and some history to go off of, we can start making a plan as to how we're going to solve our waste problem.

This is a war that everyone is fighting, and if we want to win, we must be smart about things. The best place to start, is to ask questions.

The first question to ask is:

"What waste do I or my family generate?"

Not an easy task if you remember back to the beginning chapters of this book. So, let's narrow it down.

We need to start by identifying a problem that we don't know the solution to, but is within our realm of control. Something we can affect change on. Let's start our plan by saying we want to focus on what's in our garbage can.

So, the answer to the question "What waste do I or my family generate?", is the waste in my garbage can.

This doesn't get us very far, so let's ask another question:

"Where is this problem occurring?"

It may seem like a weird and obvious question, but follow along.

"Where is this problem occurring?" in my kitchen

Let's ask and answer a few more questions.

"When was the problem first observed?" For the last few months

"How much or to what extent is the problem?" has been overflowing

"What is the problem?" causing my waste collection bin lid to be open instead of closed resulting in an added fee from the waste management service.

Now that we've asked some questions to get more detail, we have what's called a problem statement. By having a problem statement, we can focus more on a fixing a single issue, rather than trying to fix our world of problems.

So here's my problem statement I worked with. "The waste in my garbage can in my kitchen, for the last few months, has been overflowing, causing my waste collection bin lid to be open instead of closed resulting in an added fee from the waste management service."

So why is this important? Why start with a problem statement? This narrows down what you're looking at. Instead of looking at the waste I'm reusing, recovering, substituting or eliminating, I'm specifically concerned with what's in my garbage can.

Instead of worrying about my garbage can at work, in my vehicle, or even in my bathrooms, I'm focused on my kitchen garbage can. Instead of looking back years or since the time I bought my house, I'm only looking back a few months.

And finally, I'm identifying what the problem or "damage" is to me, **personally**. There it is! What I've harped about! Why is it important? It's costing me extra money.

The Math of the Problem

So now we have the problem statement. We know what the problem is, and why it's important, now we need to figure out how big or extensive the problem is. We need to measure what the current status of our problem is.

So, let's look at your garbage can in the kitchen. We need to identify what's going into it, and how much of each item is in there. This isn't super difficult. Just pay attention and maybe keep a list on your phone to track what you threw away.

Look for things such as leftover food scraps, junk mail, pop cans, water bottles, plastic packaging, pop boxes, paper plates, plastic cups, plastic forks, and plastic spoons. This will likely be the bulk of the contents in your garbage can.

So, you've identified what's in your garbage, but how much? You don't have to be super accurate, but you'll want to have a clear understanding of how much of each waste is in there, so pay attention to what is thrown away. Watch for a week to a month to get a good estimate on what you generate as waste.

Collect your data, and categorize your wastes. You need to drill down to the specifics if you want to enact sustainable changes in your life. Once you know your wastes, you need to put a number to them.

There's different numbers you can use such as how much the items cost, how much volume they take up in your garbage, or even how often you generate that waste. Regardless of the number format you use, make sure it applies to all your different wastes.

Once you have some numbers, you can rank your wastes from largest to smallest. This will give you a very specific focus, and starting at the biggest number will give you the most reduction for your efforts. Ask yourself, **"What is the ranking of your measurements?"**

Personal Story: I did this at my home and found some surprising information. Pop boxes only amounted to one or two every two weeks. Pop cans amounted to about a dozen per week. Junk mail was about a dozen envelopes a week. Water and pop bottles were only 2 or 3 a week. Plastic packaging was less than a dozen per week. Turns out we don't drink a lot of pop.

Then I noticed that with every dinner, we were throwing away enough food scraps to generally make another plate for dinner. This caught my attention. We were throwing away on average around a plate of food every time we sat down for a meal.

But then I noticed the dishes. To prepare those meals, we were averaging 7 paper plates per day. Looking at forks and spoons was a little more difficult, so I did some math. I looked at how many forks came in the boxes that we'd buy, and multiplied that by how many boxes we typically bought in a year, which came out to 1500 forks and spoons per year.

Now of course is wasn't an exact number, but it's enough for me to understand the scope of the usage. We use a lot of single use disposable forks, spoons and paper plates. Plastic cups added to the single use disposable count, coming in at around 960 per year. I had found my bulk. Single use items.

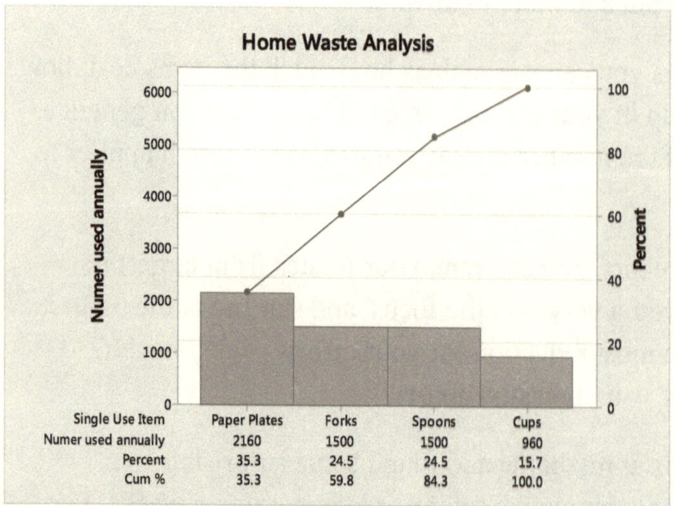

So, you've found your problem, and measured how big of a problem it is. What do you do now?

Now's the time to evaluate and come up with solutions. Now you need to start working down the steps in the waste hierarchy pyramid.

Finding Your Solution

Now it's time to ask yourself some questions. The ability to ask yourself questions, and come up with your own answers is vital to being able to eliminate waste. It can be difficult sometimes to know what questions to ask, so stick to the pyramid and ask these questions. Make sure you answer each question as precisely as possible.

"Can I eliminate this waste from my life?"

"Can I use something else so I don't have to generate this waste?"

"Is there a way I can cut back on how much of this waste I generate?"

"Can I use this waste for something else, even if only temporary?"

"Can I recycle this waste?"

"Can I burn this waste?"

There's a lot to be considered here, and which is why measuring your waste is so important. If you answer a question with a no, move on to the next. If you answer no to all the questions, ask again. Asking yourself a second time can cause you to think a little deeper and maybe think of something that turns that no into a yes.

If your answer is yes, don't be content with that answer. It's a good answer to have, but you need to look a little deeper or you might end up doing something that could cause you pain down the road.

If you answer yes, then ask yourself, How? How can you eliminate the waste? How can you Substitute for something else? How can you reduce your generation of the waste?

Let's take a quick look at all of the pyramid questions on the assumption that you answer yes, and ask some follow up questions.

"Can I eliminate this waste from my life?" Yes

1. **"How will I eliminate this waste?"**
2. **"Are there negative effects to eliminating this waste?"**
3. **"How will I overcome or adapt to the negative effects?"**
4. **"Do the negatives outweigh the benefit for me?"**

"Can I use something else so I don't have to generate this waste?" Yes

1. **"How will I substitute this waste?"**
2. **"Are there negative effects to substituting this waste?"**
3. **"How will I overcome or adapt to the negative effects?"**
4. **"Do the negatives outweigh the benefit for me?"**

"Is there a way I can cut back on how much of this waste I generate? Yes

1. **"How will I reduce this waste?"**
2. **"Are there negative effects to reducing this waste?"**
3. **"How will I overcome or adapt to the negative effects?"**

    4. "Do the negatives outweigh the benefit for me?"

"Can I use this waste for something else, even if only temporary?" Yes

1. "How will I reuse this waste?"
2. "Are there negative effects to reusing this waste?"
3. "How will I overcome or adapt to the negative effects?"
4. "Do the negatives outweigh the benefit for me?"

"Can I recycle this waste?" Yes

1. "How will I recycle this waste?"
2. "Are there negative effects to recycling this waste?"
3. "How will I overcome or adapt to the negative effects?"
4. "Do the negatives outweigh the benefit for me?"

"Can I burn or compost this waste?" Yes

1. "How will I recover this waste?"
2. "Are there negative effects to recovering this waste?"
3. "How will I overcome or adapt to the negative effects?"
4. "Do the negatives outweigh the benefit for me?"

As you can see, it's not as open and shut of a case as you may think to identifying a possible solution. There may be other questions you want to ask as well, but these should give you enough information to confidently make a decision that you can stand behind if someone asks you "Why are you doing that?"

Implementing Your Decision

Now that you've worked thru the questions and decided on an action, it's time to implement your decision. You should be able to feel confidant and secure, with a feeling that you know what you're doing. This will help you to be able to commit to your actions, and not lose sight of what you intend to do.

It may seem easy, and seem like you should "Just do it", and chances are you're right. Take the leap into whatever actions you came up with, and follow through. Once you've taken that leap and implemented your improvement, you need to make sure you can sustain and control the situation so the problem doesn't arise again.

Here's an example: I identified that I was throwing away over 2,000 plates a year. This was costing me almost $300 per year. I decided that I want to eliminate this waste by using regular dishes, and no longer buying paper plates.

This will increase the number of dishes I must wash, averaging 7 plates per day each week. This is estimated to increase the number of dish washer loads I currently do to 5 loads per week.

I currently buy bulk packs of dishwasher detergent, and will create a chore chart item to schedule starting a dish load before bed every night on weeknights.

I already start a load of dishes almost every day, and scheduling to do a load before bed on weekdays will not take any significant amount of time, nor will the noise keep me awake.

If you notice what I've done here, I've managed to create a detailed and concise plan for how I want to deal with my waste issue. I've focused the scope of my problem all the way down to paper plates, and created a plan for how I will improve or fix the issue.

This is great, but we're not quite done yet. There's still one more thing to do if we want to fully solve our waste problem, "move on".

Just because you eliminate or reduce your largest waste, doesn't mean you're done. Here's where your scoring of issues really come in to play. Since you've knocked down your largest waste, a new waste has stepped up to take its place on the leader board.

Continuing with the example, the next waste on the list is plastic forks. Now things are starting to get a little easier. We already have a lot of work into identifying our wastes and solutions, so now we need to consolidate solutions.

We need to ask another question here:

"Is my action universal to other wastes?"

What do I mean by that? Are there any other wastes that you have, that can be solved with the actions already identified?

Can forks go in the dish washer? Yes

Can spoons go in the dish washer? Yes

Can cups go in the dish washer? Yes

Can food scraps go in the dish washer? NO

Any time you can answer yes to the universal question, you can skip over most of the rest of the analysis, but you should ask yourself yet one more question:

"Will including other waste into my decision, change my action?"

By this I mean, will adding all those items increase the number of dish washer loads I will have to do. If yes, I may need to re-evaluate the negatives, how to overcome the negatives, and if the benefits still outweigh the negatives.

It all depends on you, and what you're willing to do to accomplish your waste reduction goals. This may seem like a lot. A lot of questions, a lot of analysis, a lot of measuring, and it is, but it's effective.

If you're willing to go through all the work to properly assess and improve your waste, chances are you'll follow thru with it and stick with it. It's not likely that anyone will put in all the work, just to say "it's not worth it.

I don't want things to be confusing, and seem like it's too much work. Who wants to rifle thru pages in a book to try and find all the questions you need to ask? No one, and it'd be stupid of me to assume anyone would, so, I've created a checklist.

The list, at the end of this book, will walk you through all of the questions we've asked. Simply answer them to the best of your abilities, and you'll be able to make a difference in your generation of waste.

83

The Brighter Sides of Business

Improving your Restaurant

As you can see, solving our waste is not going to be easy. While the last section of this book focused on your garbage can in the kitchen, the principles apply to everywhere. Now let's look a little more at the business level, and some things you can do to fight the waste war. Remember, ask the question from the previous section, they will apply to your business as well.

Do you run a restaurant? If so, how much food waste do you have every single day, and how much of that food waste is still edible food? If you say none, you may not be being honest with yourself.

You may want to think about setting up a compost bin in your kitchen for vegetable scraps, and find someone to take it for you. This can help you cut way back on your waste generation.

Maybe think about changing your straws. Moving to paper straws will reduce plastic and give a little buzz, but if you moved to silicone that can be washed and reused, you'll generate a LOT of buzz, and should be able to reduce the cost of supplies over time.

Do you sell specialty coffees? Sell reusable mugs with a promotion that anyone who brings their own mugs gets a certain amount off their bill. You'll make far more revenue from the mugs than you'll lose from the discount, and think of it as free advertising. People will see your mugs around town, so make them look awesome.

Offer a **"Doggy Bag"** promotion. Put a flier in your window or otherwise advertise a discount on a customer's meal if they bring their own Tupperware for leftovers. A 5% discount shouldn't eat into your profits to much.

Even better than the doggy bag promotion, sell your customers Tupperware containers with your logo on it for their leftovers. Yet another wat to make a little extra money, or offset the discount if you run both options.

Napkins are simple, change out your paper napkins with cloth ones. This is simple to do and will increase your "quality". Customers will unknowingly start associating you as a nicer, higher quality restaurant.

Sugar and cream are another easy one. Just put sugar in a shaker and leave it on the table. It's commonly thought that customers will use less if it's in individual packages, but once a they get done ripping open six or seven packages for a single cup of coffee, it kind of defeats that idea.

Same with cream, keep some full creamer pots on hand if you have room in the fridge, or fill them when a customer orders coffee. Non-dairy creamer doesn't technically even need to be refrigerated, but you may want to do so anyway just for the customers perception. Not everyone will know it's perfectly fine for it to set out.

Being known as a waste free restaurant may be difficult, but if you put a little brain power to it, it's fully doable. The biggest problem is going to be food left on the customers plate, but there's a solution for that as well.

Hog feed. It may not sound great, but "swill" is feed that contains meat. Swill may not be the most popular type of feed due to the potential for disease in the pigs, but this is rare, and largely only contracted from uncooked or undercooked meat.

If you want to go this route, make sure you talk to a hog farmer and discuss what scraps they will allow before just dumping it all together. Some farmers may be ok with it, but that's a discussion you'd have to have with them.

Becoming known as the first "Waste Free" restaurant in your area is possible, and it would not only be a HUGE accomplishment, but would really be a great way to promote your restaurant.

The Grocery Store Potential

Do you run a grocery store or even work at one? There's many things you can do to improve you waste output. The one that most every store does, is offer reusable bags, and some even encourage this by charging for plastic bags.

Not a bad start, but why not have a promotion where you give away a free reusable bag with a purchase of $100 or more? You'll be out a small amount of money, but you'll likely make it back when people come in to buy more bags.

Run the promotion for a month and you'll have a lot more people wanting to buy more bags. The ease and convenience for the customer of a reusable bag is great, and people forget their bags so often that they'll realize they need more than one or two. I, like many others I know, have at least two dozen so we can always keep a set in our vehicles.

What about your meat scraps? Do you throw them in the trash? Instead of tossing them, talk to the local butcher and see if they'd want to buy your scraps from you, if not, see if they'd take them as donation. It may not make you any money, but it will save you on waste and may be able to help cut down on your disposal fees.

Same with your produce department. Why throw away perfectly edible produce when there may be a local farmer that may want them for feed or compost. Put a flier up in your window to catch the attention of anyone who would be interested in buying discarded produce as feed.

Don't live somewhere that a farmer will see your flier? Check with the local homeless shelters and food banks to see if they would be able to accept the edible produce that won't sell on your shelves.

What about all the prepackaged items in your store? Talk to your distributors. Tell them you're looking to reduce your waste, and ask them if they have any alternative packaging.

If not, maybe it will spark them to considering alternatives. Perhaps they can ship your goods in reusable shipping crates, that you return the next time you receive a delivery.

Maybe you're able to take after a well know store that doesn't even use bags, but instead provide boxes for customers. This allows them to be environmentally conscious by reducing their waste and reusing their shipping boxes.

If you run a store, then you know that strategic placement of items is critical, so why not set up a stand at the beginning of the produce section selling mesh vegetable bags? Put these on display where everyone who enters your store HAS to pass by them to get to fresh produce.

The deli is another place in your store where you can make improvements and money doing so. Instead of only using Styrofoam cups and little plastic bags for your deli items, offer your customers a Tupperware container for a small fee?

You can make some money from the container sale, and your customer may feel rewarded because they just got a piece of reusable Tupperware with their food.

Reward your customers by rewarding yourself, and before long you'll have a very nice cyclical rewards system going that can drive up business without many people even realizing it.

The Others

There's so many different types of companies out there, that it'd be impossible to describe reduction actions for everyone. On the flip side of that, there's something that can be done by everyone. Every company has waste, be it physical or process waste.

All it takes is a little thought and ingenuity to come up with some amazing ideas. For instance, do you manufacture a product such as coffee? Start using glass jars or burlap sacks instead of plastic packages.

Do you sell office supplies? Offer non-plastic bulk packaging for items typically shipped in clamshell packaging. A simple little box with an image of the product will do just fine in most cases.

Do you ship product using plastic air pockets or Styrofoam packaging peanuts to keep the product safe? Us brown packaging paper instead. It takes up less storage space and can provide better protection than either plastic options.

Maybe you're not a manufacturer, maybe you're a company that doesn't sell a product, but sells a service. Are you making sure that your employees and coworkers are aware of recycling or better yet, waste elimination?

Many people think that they know everything they need to know about waste management, just because they throw that pop bottle into the blue bin, but if you're reading this section of this book, it's likely you learned, you might not know as much as you thought.

But you don't have to be an expert in waste management to be able to make a change.

Personal Story: Prior to 2017, I knew next to nothing about environmental issues. I didn't recycle, and I never paid attention to my waste. I could drive by a mound of garbage that collected under an overpass, and not even register in my brain having ever seen it.

But I'm not unique. Until I started getting involved with environmental issues, I was like most of the people in my community. But then I got a new position as the chairman of our company's waste and energy reduction committee.

I knew nothing, and never had any formal training in environmental issues, but what I did have, was a strong interest in process waste reduction. When I got the position, I set to work.

I researched waste reduction night and day, learning more and more about the environmental side of things. I learned about recycling, and waste to energy, and I learned how to eliminate waste in processes.

I combined the two areas and began an awareness campaign at the company to inform others about issues that were prevalent in our community and around the world, but that almost no one had any interest in.

The more I learned, and the more I dealt with waste and recycling management centers around my area, the more I learned how broken we were. Most people think of recycling as the go to for cleaning up the environment, and it's not.

How We "Level Up"

Disclaimer: In this final section of the book, there is likely a comment that will make some people mad. I would apologize in advance, but where's the fun in that. You'll know it when you read it, but keep reading.

Recycling can help, but it will never be the cure all we so desperately need. We need to go to the source of the waste generating processes, and curb the generation at the start.

This is what a lot of environmentalists try to elude to, but in my opinion, they get too angry when people challenge their views, and make things worse, creating a bad taste in the mouth when some people hear the term environmentalist. So why are they challenged? Because not everyone views things the same way.

People picket large waste producing companies, trying to shame them into "doing the right thing", but all that does is create a backlash of anger and spite. Companies feel attacked, so they dig in their heels. Environmentalists feel ignored, so they argue harder. And the cycle of anger and mistrust ensues.

Solving Our Waste: The War On Us

We need to realize that everyone is trying to make a living, and wants to live in the most comfortable manner they can. Environmentalists have a duty to clean up and save the world, while companies have a duty to make a profit.

They don't have to be two different or colliding methodologies, and can play pretty nicely with each other. Environmentalists should typically have a great deal of knowledge around environmental issues, and can actually help companies come up with ways to improve their business.

Likewise, businesses are good at making money, and can provide a comfortable living for environmentalists under their employ. It takes working together to make a difference.

One thing both sides need to understand, is that each side is doing what they think is best. Maybe you're a company that already employs the talents and knowledge of one or more environmentally minded people, but you still get picketed.

You have someone, or maybe even a team that is actively working on making your company more environmentally friendly, but people don't know what you're doing. Miscommunication can lead to a huge disconnect between the company, and the environmentalists.

Now, as for just recycling…**Recycling Sucks!** I despise recycling, although I can see the benefit in the practice, and do recycle what I can. Recycling, in my opinion, is a poorly applied band-aid that convinced people we were doing the right thing, so that we didn't have to do the right thing.

Recycling is a hyper complicated process that takes the dedication of EVERY member of society to CONTINUOUSLY be vigilant in making sure they know not only the current process, but the market for what is selling as well.

That's why we're in the mess we are in, because it's next to impossible for EVERYONE on the planet to get on board, and even if everyone was onboard, we as a society, are not advanced enough to deal effectively with all of the many waste streams that exist.

We demonize plastic as the worst waste in the world, but without it we wouldn't be even close to as advanced as we are. Can we live without single use plastic? Most people will say "of course, we can, we did for thousands of years!" I beg to differ.

If we want to continue living in the advancements we've made over the last 100 years or so, we need single use plastic. We can live without plastic bottles or plastic shopping bags, but some items such as some packaging of products, would seriously upheave our society. Plastics not a demon material, we just have become too complacent with how we use it.

So, if I don't like recycling, and I don't think plastic is the most horrible invention to plague mankind, what do I believe is the way to win the war we have launched on ourselves?

How do we reach that next level of innovation that's going to save our world? The answers simple, yet exceedingly complicated, and we've been working through it this entire time. The pyramid.

We have the answer, the waste hierarchy. We need to focus more on starting at the top, and working our way down. Eliminate! That's my biggest deal. If we want to improve, we have to eliminate.

Recycling won't work, waste to energy destroys in order to create, landfills bury our shame. We have to eliminate, and we have to do it together. No more yelling or arguing with each other. We need to help each other come up with new awesome ways to solve our waste problem.

If you follow the questions as laid out to you, it will put you on the right path to eliminating your waste. But remember one thing, in this book, we've only been talking about physical, municipal waste. There's dozens of other types of waste out there. Hazardous waste, Bio-Hazardous Waste, Chemical waste, carbon footprint or emissions waste, process waste, and so on.

We want to solve our waste, but we need to walk before we can run. Take care of your personal waste. Eliminate what you can, substitute, reduce, and reuse what you can. Recycle if you really know that what your putting in the bin is truly going to be recycled.

Maybe leave burning to the professionals, or save your cardboard boxes for the next bonfire. Whatever you do, you need to solve and control your contribution to the waste problem, if you want to start making a difference. This comment goes all the way up to the highest-level CEO of your company too.

I'm not saying you have to live a zero-waste life to be successful. Despite the claims, I know of no one who has truly achieved zero waste. Just do what you can.

If you have sway in your workplace, try to work with people and educate them in a rewarding way. Buy your coworkers doughnuts and watch a documentary on the great pacific garbage patch. Start a little group inside your organization to sit down once a week or month and have a quick discussion about ways to improve your business.

You don't have to do a lot, and you don't have to get upset with those who feel differently than you do. Find a common ground where you can benefit from each other.

I know I got a little preachy here at the end, but we really do need to follow the path we have already laid out for ourselves. The process is there, we just need to pay attention and think.

I don't consider myself an environmentalist, I'm just me. And me thinks that we need to think more about having better thinks. **THAT,** is how we solve our waste.

The Obligatory Thank You

Thank You for reading my book. If you liked this book, and even if you didn't, please leave me a review. I encourage questions, corrections, and any type of feedback. Positive or Negative.

Hopefully you learned a few things. If so, check out some of my other books where I help take you thru learning different topics from the beginner lever, and give you the keys to your own development.

Waste Elimination Questions

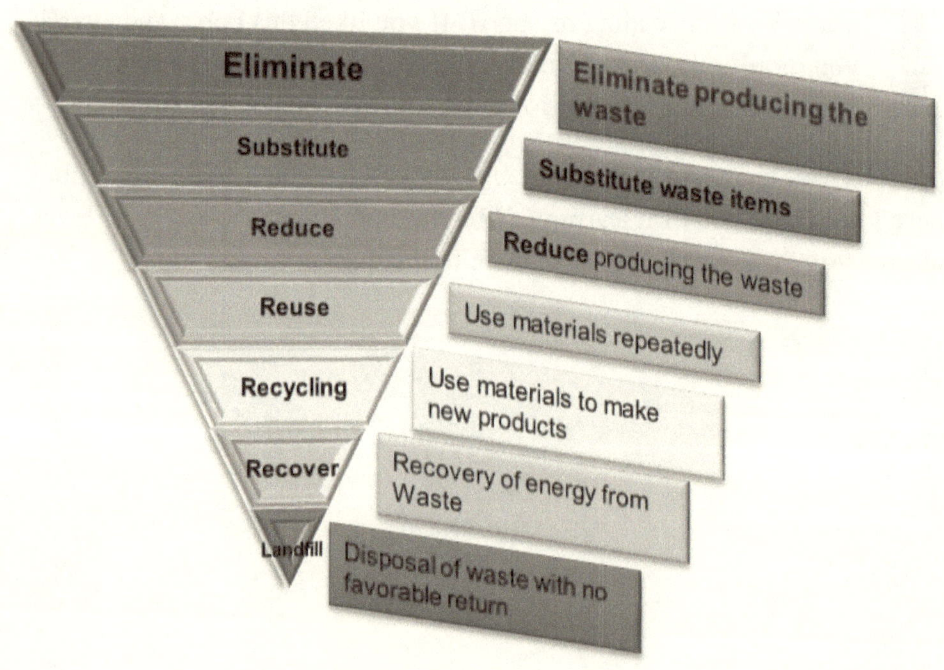

DEFINE YOUR WASTE

WHAT WASTE DO YOU GENERATE?
WHERE IS THIS PROBLEM OCCURRING?
HOW LONG HAS THIS PROBLEM BEEN OBSERVED?
TO WHAT EXTENT IS THE PROBLEM?
WHY IS THIS A PROBLEM?
WHAT IS YOUR PROBLEM STATEMENT?   *(Combine all your previous answers into one statement)*

MEASURE YOUR WASTE

WHAT IS THE RANKING OF YOUR MEASUREMENTS?

ANALYZE YOUR WASTE

CAN YOU ELIMINATE YOUR WASTE?
HOW WILL YOU ELIMINATE YOUR WASTE?
ARE THERE NEGATIVE EFFECTS TO ELIMINATING THIS WASTE?
HOW WILL YOU OVERCOME THE NEGATIVE EFFECTS?
DO THE NEGATIVES OUTWEIGH THE BENEFITS?
CAN YOU SUBSTITUTE YOUR WASTE?
HOW WILL YOU SUBSTITUTE YOUR WASTE?
ARE THERE NEGATIVE EFFECTS TO SUBSTITUTING THIS WASTE?
HOW WILL YOU OVERCOME THE NEGATIVE EFFECTS?
DO THE NEGATIVES OUTWEIGH THE BENEFITS?

CAN YOU REDUCE YOUR WASTE?
HOW WILL YOU REDUCE YOUR WASTE?
ARE THERE NEGATIVE EFFECTS TO REDUCING THIS WASTE?
HOW WILL YOU OVERCOME THE NEGATIVE EFFECTS?
DO THE NEGATIVES OUTWEIGH THE BENEFITS?
CAN YOU REUSE YOUR WASTE?
HOW WILL YOU REUSE YOUR WASTE?
ARE THERE NEGATIVE EFFECTS TO REUSING THIS WASTE?
HOW WILL YOU OVERCOME THE NEGATIVE EFFECTS?
DO THE NEGATIVES OUTWEIGH THE BENEFITS?
CAN YOU RECYCLE YOUR WASTE?
HOW WILL YOU RECYCLE YOUR WASTE?

ARE THERE NEGATIVE EFFECTS TO RECYCLING THIS WASTE?
HOW WILL YOU OVERCOME THE NEGATIVE EFFECTS?
DO THE NEGATIVES OUTWEIGH THE BENEFITS?

IMPROVE YOUR WASTE

WHAT OTHER WASTE IS YOUR IMPROVEMENT ACTION UNIVERSAL TO?
Will including other waste into my decision, change my action plan?